All Kinds of Friends, Even Green!

Written & Photographed by Ellen B. Senisi

WOODBINE HOUSE 2002

YAHOO! I'm going to school—gotta see my friends!

There's Kate next door getting ready for school, too.

She's saying good-bye to Zaki.

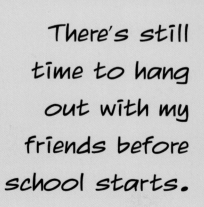

Great!

There's still time to hang out with my friends before school starts.

"Hi, Moses," says Kaila, "Give me five!"

"Good morning, class!"

says my teacher, Ms. Bird. "You'll be writing about friends today.

A friend is someone you know very well and like very much."

But there are lots of people I know well and like very much—
so where am I supposed to start?

I could write about Jimmy.

We tell secrets and say funny things.

I could
write about
playing with
Manuel
and how
we like
to go

fast.

And then there's Jocelyn.

She knows what it's like to be in a wheelchair like me.

I do like being in this class and having all these friends to hang around with.
But everyone else will write about them—I'm going to do something different.

When Mrs. Izzo asks, "Moses, do you need help?"

I say no, I need time to think.

And so I think.

I think about how grownups can be friends, too.

There's my mom and dad, of course. We laugh together. We love each other so much. But that's not what I want to write about today.

Now how about a teacher?

I wonder if anyone else will write about that.

My other teacher, Ms. Janik, acts like a friend sometimes. We talk about things. I tell her we need to go have a burger and fries and relax.

And, of course,

there's my neighbor, Kate.

She's a teenager and she can drive!

She has two pet iguanas.

We have a blast when she babysits for me.

"Class, it's sounding a little noisy,"

says Ms. Bird.

"Remember that this is time for writing about friends, not talking to them."

And then I think of something definitely different:

animals can be friends, too.

I could say that Kate's pet iguanas are my friends.

Hashi is a boy and Zaki is a girl. But what could I say about them? They're cute, but why do I like them?

Well,

I especially like Zaki.

She doesn't have any toes on her back feet, like Hashi does.

Kate says Zaki is her iguana with special needs.

Zaki's toes were poisoned by mites and fell off. Mites are tiny bugs that suck iguanas' blood.

Zaki had the mites when Kate brought her home from the pet store, but she didn't know it.

"Sometimes things like that just happen," says Kate.

She told me that, at first,
Zaki couldn't move around easily
because of her toes.

Kate says toes are really
important to iguanas.

She showed me how Hashi uses his
toes to climb everywhere.

But Zaki
kept trying
and trying.

Her front legs got
very strong.

Now she can
pull herself
places she
couldn't
get to
before.

I think that's what I really like about Zaki.

She figures out how to get where she wants to be in different ways than Hashi does.

She's like me.

I like Zaki and I think she likes me back.

She's the one I'm going to write about!

"Moses, that's a very empty paper!"
says Mrs. Izzo.

But I tell her, "Don't worry.
I've got it now!"

I am lucky because
I have so many friends.

I want to tell you now
about one of my friends.
She may seem different to
you at first because she is
small and green and has
little spikes on her back.
She doesn't have all her
toes, either.
But even though she
looks different than me,
something inside her is
the same as me.
And we like each other.

That is what I think being
friends is all about.

disabilities

Moses and some of the children in his class have disabilities. This means they cannot do some things other kids their own age can do. Children with disabilities may not be able to walk, speak, read, or hear. There are many kinds of disabilities. Sometimes you can see right away if someone has a disability, because he or she might use sign language to speak or perhaps be in a wheelchair, like Moses or Jocelyn. Sometimes, though, people have disabilities that are inside their bodies and can't be seen.

Disabilities are caused by problems with the body or brain. People can be born with disabilities, as Moses was. Or, like Zaki, they might get them through an accident or illness. Having special needs means, as it does for Zaki and Moses, working in different ways to do what you want or need to do.

Jocelyn uses her wheelchair inside and out to move around.

Jocelyn can't keep her hand raised for long because her muscles are weak, so a friend helps her.

Jocelyn has a special desk that's easier for her to write on than a regular school desk.

Moses

Moses is seven years old. His favorite color is red and his favorite holiday is Halloween. He likes to do play wrestling and he loves surprises. His favorite places to go are out for a burger and fries, to the park, and to go fishing. He likes to tell the story about how a fish almost pulled him into the water. He likes to read but says, "I like books about things like dinosaurs and bones, not the kind my mother always gets for me." He says he sometimes dreams that he is running in gym class and wonders what it would really be like.

Moses was born with several disabilities. He has *spina bifida* and *sacral agenesis*. His spine is not completely formed. He has problems with certain organs, too. (Organs are what you call some of the things inside your body that make it work, like your heart, stomach, lungs, and liver.) Moses was born with some of his organs missing and with some in the wrong places. This means he has to go to the doctor a lot, but the rest of the time he goes to school, watches movies, and has fun with his family and friends.

iguanas

Kate wants everyone to know that iguanas are a lot of work and only people who are ready to spend a lot of time taking good care of them should get iguanas.

Iguanas don't make any noise and they don't bite. They may scratch when you hold them, but it's not on purpose—it's just because their nails are so long. They are very shy, gentle animals. They are usually not very tame unless they have been handled gently and held a lot when they were young.

You can't miss that bright iguana-green color. Their color does change, though, depending on their mood, the weather, and their diet. Iguanas love fresh vegetables, hate days without sun, and miss their owners when they are away.

Iguanas like to hide. They often go deep under or high on top of things to sleep. Zaki likes to sleep in the back of Kate's closet, on top of the row of hangers

with clothes on them. Hashi sleeps on a high shelf with shoes and bags on it. However, he has also slept balanced on the top of Kate's door while it was open, as well as hanging from a calendar on her wall. Sometimes Zaki and Hashi hide out for a day or so. Several times Kate had to take her whole room apart to find Zaki when she didn't come out.